the ELF on the SHELF®

a Christmas tradition ™

ORCHARD BOOKS

First published in Great Britain in 2018 by The Watts Publishing Group

1 3 5 7 9 10 8 6 4 2

® and © 2018 CCA and B, LLC. All Rights Reserved.
Licensed by Rocket Licensing Ltd

Additional images © Shutterstock

A CIP catalogue record for this book is available from the British Library

ISBN 978 1 40835 907 5

Printed and bound in Slovakia

MIX
Paper from
responsible sources
FSC® C104740
FSC
www.fsc.org

Orchard Books
An imprint of Hachette Children's Group
Part of The Watts Publishing Group Limited
Carmelite House
50 Victoria Embankment
London EC4Y 0DZ

An Hachette UK Company
www.hachette.co.uk

www.hachettechildrens.co.uk

Adult supervision is recommended when glue, paint,
scissors and other sharp points are in use.

BUMPER ACTIVITY BOOK

the
ELF
on the
SHELF®

a Christmas tradition ™

THIS BOOK BELONGS TO:

callan and
♢ Olivia

MCcor mack

MEET THE SCOUT ELVES!

It is their job to watch over you in the weeks before Christmas and report back to Father Christmas. To welcome the Scout Elves into your family, you first need to give them names! Can you name these Elves?

MY NAME IS :	MY NAME IS :
....	....

My Name Is :

....

My Name Is :

....

SPECIAL SCOUT ELF POST

The Scout Elves have left two secret messages for you! Can you read the letters using the code below?

KEY:

A B C D E F G H I J K L M N

O P Q R S T U V W X Y Z

ANSWERS ON PAGE 64

HOME FOR THE NIGHT

The Scout Elves need to find their way to the North Pole to see Father Christmas! Can you help them find the route through the maze?

Start

FINISH

SANTA'S NORTH POLE
MAILROOM
WORKSHOP

9

ANSWERS ON PAGE 64

HIDDEN WORDS

The Scout Elves have hidden eight words
in this wordsearch. Can you find them all?

- Christmas
- Presents
- Tree
- Cookies
- Wreath
- Elves
- Baubles
- Candy canes

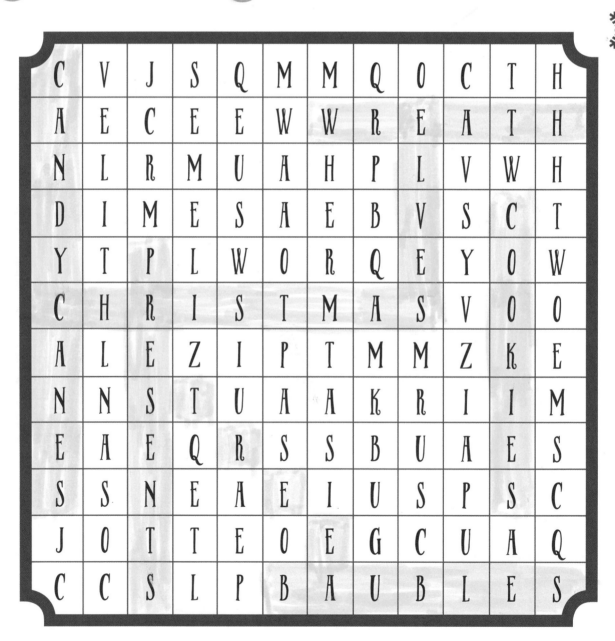

C	V	J	S	Q	M	M	Q	O	C	T	H
A	E	C	E	E	W	W	R	E	A	T	H
N	L	R	M	U	A	H	P	L	V	W	H
D	I	M	E	S	A	E	B	V	S	C	T
Y	T	P	L	W	O	R	Q	E	Y	O	W
C	H	R	I	S	T	M	A	S	V	O	O
A	L	E	Z	I	P	T	M	M	Z	K	E
N	N	S	T	U	A	A	K	R	I	I	M
E	A	E	Q	R	S	S	B	U	A	E	S
S	S	N	E	A	E	I	U	S	P	S	C
J	O	T	T	E	O	E	G	C	U	A	Q
C	C	S	L	P	B	A	U	B	L	E	S

Answers on page 64

SNACK TIME!

It's so much fun to make and decorate special Christmas biscuits! Add lots of fun toppings to the biscuits below.

COUNT THE TREATS

The Scout Elves have left lots of sweet treats for you. How many of each item can you count? Write the numbers in the boxes.

CHRISTMAS BISCUITS = ◯

CANDY CANES = ◯

SWEETS = ◯

HOT CHOCOLATE = ◯

ANSWERS ON PAGE 64

FUN IN THE SNOW

It's time to build a snowman! Can you spot five differences between the two scenes?

ANSWERS ON PAGE 64

CHRISTMAS WISH LIST

What do you wish for this year? Use these pages to write and draw everything you hope for this Christmas.

PRETTY DECORATIONS

Decorate the Christmas baubles in lots of bright, festive colours!

COLOUR IN THE SCENE!

COPY AND DRAW

Copy the drawing of the Scout Elf square by square into the grid on the right. Then colour him in!

Name your Scout Elf! ....

LET'S DECORATE!

The Scout Elves are ready to hang the wreath.
Finish it off with lots of festive colours!

Design your own wreath below. What will you decorate it with – holly, baubles, ivy or beads?

COLOUR IN THE SCENE!

HELPING HAND

The night before Christmas is very busy for Father Christmas, he needs lots of help from his Scout Elves and Elf Pets® Reindeer. Colour in his helpers then name all nine of his original reindeer!

1 ....

2 ....

3 ....

4 ....

5 ....

6 ....

7 ....

8 ....

9 ....

COLOUR IN
THE SCENE!

COLOUR IN THE SCENE!

WRAP IT UP

These helpful Scout Elves are wrapping presents to go under the tree. Colour in the Elves and their presents!

Draw some more presents here – what do
you wish for this Christmas?

HANG YOUR STOCKING

A cheeky Scout Elf and Elf Pets® Saint Bernard pup have climbed into these stockings! Add lots of colour – why not add your name?

COLOUR IN THE SCENE!

LANDING ZONE

BALLET PRACTICE

The Scout Elves love to dance and play! Can you colour in these Elves as they practise some ballet?

ON THE SHELF

This Scout Elf has just returned from the North Pole and is ready for the new day! Colour him in.

GET CREATIVE

The Scout Elves love to make up Christmas songs and poems. Can you write a song or poem below?

FIND THE SCOUT ELF!

The Scout Elves are hiding somewhere in this scene. Can you spot them? Look out for the other objects below, too!

CAN YOU FIND THESE ITEMS IN THE SCENE?

 x3 ✓

 x4 ✓

x3

 x5

HOW MANY
SCOUT ELVES
DID YOU SPOT
IN THE SCENE?

ANSWERS ON PAGE 64

TO THE NORTH POLE

Only one of these trails leads to the North Pole. Can you follow the lines to find out which one?

A

B

C

SANTA'S NORTH POLE

MAILROOM

WORKSHOP

ANSWERS ON PAGE 64

SHADOW MATCH

The Scout Elves are playing a shadow game. Can you match the picture of this Elf to his shadow?

A

B

C

D

E

ANSWERS ON PAGE 64

CHRISTMAS POST

At Christmas it's nice to send cards to your friends
and family to show you are thinking about them.
Design your own Christmas cards below.

PICK YOUR PATH

The Scout Elves are looking forward to a nice mug of hot chocolate but they need to get to the kitchen! Can you show them the way? Look out for blocked paths!

START

FINISH

ANSWERS ON PAGE 64

CHRISTMAS QUIZ

Look carefully at the Christmas items. Can you fill in the blank spaces to write what they are?

1  C a n d Y   c A N e s

2  P r E S E n t S

3  S c o u t   E l f

4  s n O W m a n

5  H o t   C h o c o L A t e

ANSWERS ON PAGE 64

SPECIAL PAPER

The Scout Elves love wrapping presents. Can you design some special wrapping paper below?

WISHES FOR THE NEW YEAR

The festive season is a good time to make some resolutions for the year ahead. Use the space below to write your New Year's Resolutions.

THIS YEAR I WILL ...

 Start a new hobby

THIS YEAR I WILL ...

Work extra hard at school

Help with some household chores

THIS YEAR I WANT TO ...

Read one new book a month

THIS YEAR I CAN ...

THIS YEAR I WILL LEARN HOW TO ...

Make a new friend

FAMILY FUN

Play this fun festive game with your family or friends!

YOU WILL NEED
- A counter per player
- A die

HOW TO PLAY

Place your counters on the number 1.

Take turns rolling the die and moving forwards the number of spaces shown.

If you land on a stocking, move up the board.

If you land on a candy cane, move down the board.

The first player to reach the North Pole wins!

CUT OUT YOUR COUNTERS!

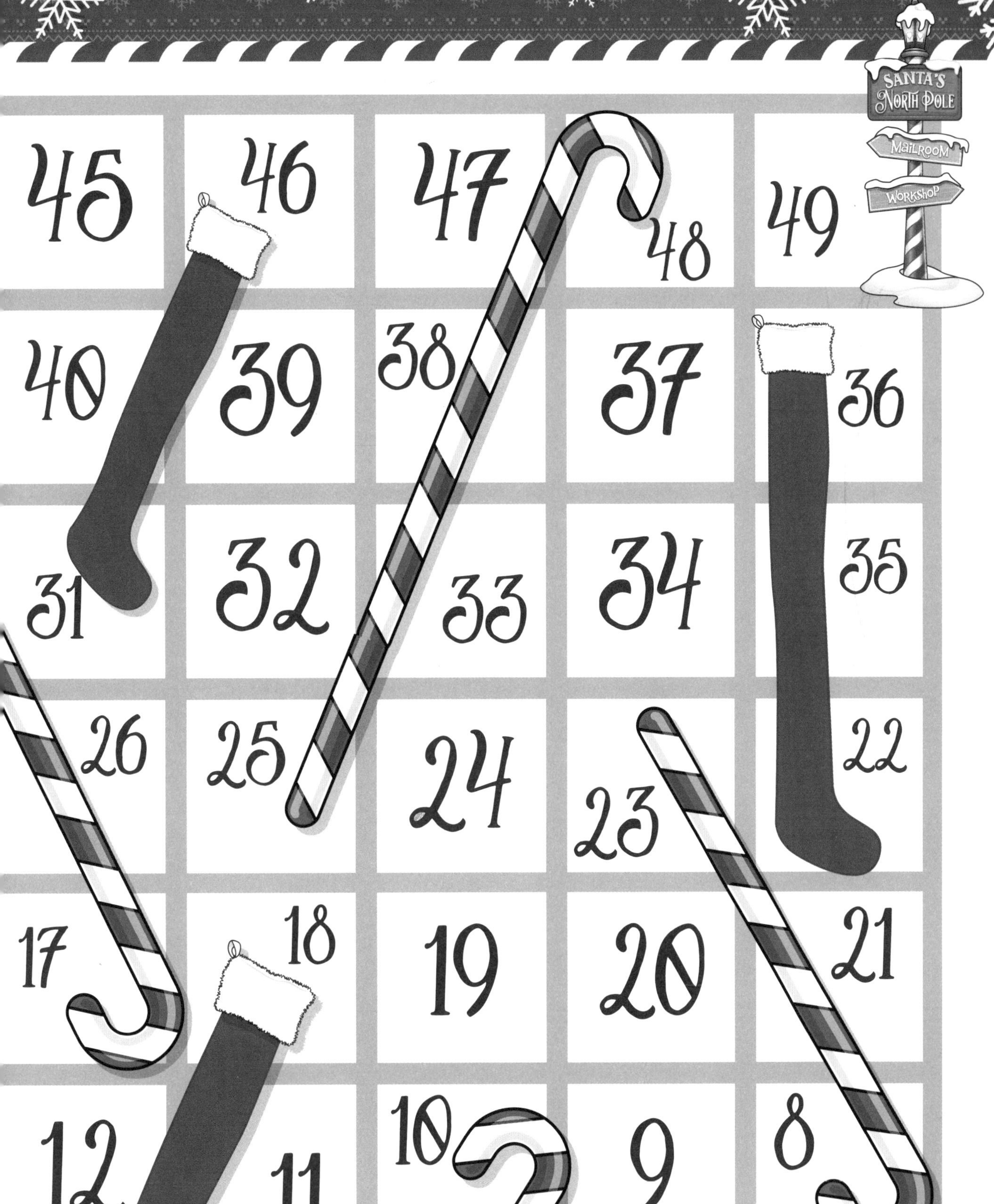

SANTA'S NORTH POLE
MAILROOM
WORKSHOP
45 46 47 48 49
40 39 38 37 36
31 32 33 34 35
26 25 24 23 22
17 18 19 20 21
12 11 10 9 8
3 4 5 6 7

FUN IN THE SNOW

It's snowing outside! No two snowflakes are ever the same, so draw lots more unique snowflakes!

COLOUR IN
THE SCENE!

49

THE NIGHT BEFORE CHRISTMAS

The night before Christmas is so exciting! The Scout Elves are making some delicious hot chocolate for Father Christmas. Colour in the scene and then draw your favourite snack to leave out for Father Christmas.

COLOUR IN THE SCENE!

COLOUR IN THE SCENE!

COLOUR IN THE SCENE!

COLOUR IN THE SCENE!

PRETTY DECORATIONS

The Scout Elves are decorating the tree in time
for Christmas. Colour in the scene!

DRAW YOUR OWN DECORATIONS FOR THE TREE!

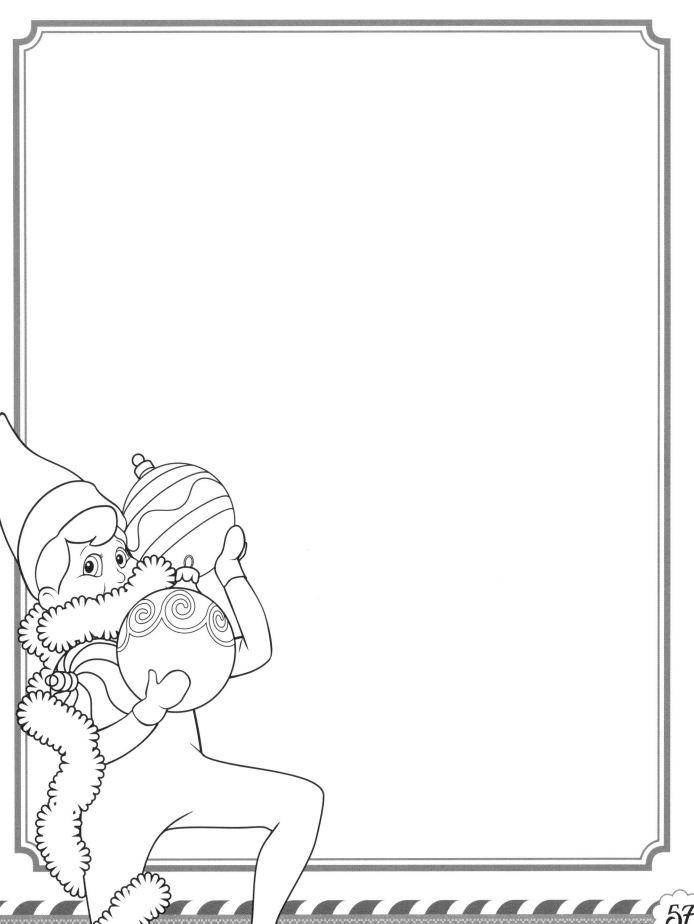

SPECIAL DELIVERY

The Scout Elves bring messages to Father Christmas.
Colour in these Elves on their way to the North Pole.
Then write a letter to Father Christmas!

DEAR FATHER CHRISTMAS,

COUNTDOWN TO CHRISTMAS

Every night, the Scout Elves travel back to the North Pole to see Father Christmas. When they return, they find a new spot for the day! Add a sticker when you have found your Scout Elf and use the chart to record their home for the day.

MY SCOUT ELF'S NAME IS

....

1ST   I found my Scout Elf!

Add Sticker!

They were hiding ...

....

....

....

2ND   I found my Scout Elf!

Add Sticker!

They were hiding ...

....

....

....

3RD   I found my Scout Elf!

Add Sticker!

They were hiding ...

....

....

....

4TH
I found my Scout Elf!

They were hiding …

....
....
....

5TH
I found my Scout Elf!

They were hiding …

....
....
....

6TH
I found my Scout Elf!

Add Sticker!

They were hiding …

....
....
....

7TH
I found my Scout Elf!

They were hiding …

....
....
....

8TH
I found my Scout Elf!

They were hiding …

....
....
....

9TH
I found my Scout Elf!

They were hiding …

....
....
....

10TH
I found my Scout Elf!

They were hiding …

....
....
....

11TH
I found my Scout Elf!

They were hiding …

....
....
....

12TH
I found my Scout Elf!

They were hiding …

....
....
....

13TH
I found my Scout Elf!

Add Sticker!

They were hiding …

....
....
....

14TH
I found my Scout Elf!

Add Sticker!

They were hiding …

....
....
....

15TH
I found my Scout Elf!

Add Sticker!

They were hiding …

....
....
....

16TH
I found my Scout Elf!

Add Sticker!

They were hiding …

....
....
....

17TH
I found my Scout Elf!

Add Sticker!

They were hiding …

....
....
....

18TH
I found my Scout Elf!

Add Sticker!

They were hiding …

....
....
....

19TH
I found my Scout Elf!

Add Sticker!

They were hiding …

....
....
....

20TH
I found my Scout Elf!

Add Sticker!

They were hiding …

....
....
....

21ST
I found my Scout Elf!

Add Sticker!

They were hiding …

....
....
....

22ND
I found my Scout Elf!

Add Sticker!

They were hiding …

....

....

23RD
I found my Scout Elf!

Add Sticker!

They were hiding …

....

....

24TH
I found my Scout Elf!

IT'S CHRISTMAS EVE!

Add Sticker!

They were hiding …

....

....

25TH
I found my Scout Elf!

IT'S CHRISTMAS DAY!

Add Sticker!

They were hiding …

....

....

ANSWERS

SPECIAL SCOUT ELF POST
Page 6 — You've been good!
Page 7 — Merry Christmas!

HOME FOR THE NIGHT
Pages 8-9

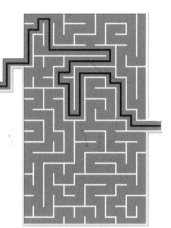

HIDDEN WORDS
Page 10

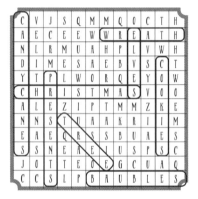

COUNT THE TREATS
Page 12
Christmas Biscuits — 7
Candy Canes — 6
Sweets — 10
Hot Chocolate — 6

FUN IN THE SNOW
Page 13

HELPING HAND
Page 23

1. Dasher	4. Vixen	7. Donner
2. Dancer	5. Comet	8. Blitzen
3. Prancer	6. Cupid	9. Rudolph

FIND THE SCOUT ELF!
Pages 34-35

There are 7 Scout Elves in the scene!

TO THE NORTH POLE
Page 36
Route B leads you to the North Pole.

SHADOW MATCH
Page 37
E is the matching shadow.

PICK YOUR PATH
Pages 40-41

CHRISTMAS QUIZ
Page 42

1 — Candy Canes	4 — Snowman
2 — Presents	5 — Hot Chocolate
3 — Scout Elf	

USE THESE STICKERS FOR PAGES 60-63